Bulletins from a War Zone

poems by

Susan Shaw Sailer

Finishing Line Press
Georgetown, Kentucky

Bulletins from a War Zone

Copyright © 2019 by Susan Shaw Sailer
ISBN 978-1-64662-077-7 First Edition
All rights reserved under International and Pan-American Copyright Conventions.
No part of this book may be reproduced in any manner whatsoever without written permission from the publisher, except in the case of brief quotations embodied in critical articles and reviews.

ACKNOWLEDGMENTS

I thank the editors of the following journals in which these poems first appeared:

"Aseel Turned Away at Airport Gate," *Switched-On Gutenberg*
"Blast or Belong," *Voices from the Attic*
"Dust, Blowing in the Wind," 2018, *Vox Populi*
 "From Raqqa Syria to Crete," *Waves: A Confluence of Women's Voices*, forthcoming, 2019.
 "How to Become an Emigrant," *WORDPEACE*
"In Zaatari," *Conclave*, "Justifying the Margins"
"My Name Is Hanan Aboulafia," *Minerva Rising*

Thanks to the following people for their help in shaping and deepening these poems: Maggie Anderson, Connie Banta, Jan Beatty and the Tuesday morning Madwomen in the Attic group at Carlow University, Roberta Feins, John Krumberger, Lynne McMahon, Tom Miles, Richard Montgomery, Liane Ellison Norman, Lori Wilson.

Publisher: Leah Maines
Editor: Christen Kincaid
Cover Art: Thomas H. Miles
Author Photo: Thomas H. Miles
Cover Design: Elizabeth Maines McCleavy

Printed in the USA on acid-free paper.
Order online: www.finishinglinepress.com
also available on amazon.com

Author inquiries and mail orders:
Finishing Line Press
P. O. Box 1626
Georgetown, Kentucky 40324
U. S. A.

Table of Contents

How to Become an Emigrant 1

At Sea with Laser Pointer 2

What He Carries with Him 3

The Field outside Homs 4

In Zaatari 5

In the Refugee Camp the Art Therapist Asks Surayya about

    Her Painting 6

Dead Man Carried Lentils from Market 7

Touching Air 8

Bulletins from a War Zone 9

The Emigrant 11

Raqqa Syria to Crete 13

Dust, Blowing in the Wind 14

In the Sahara 15

The Sahel 16

Aseel Turned Away at Airport Gate 19

My Name Is Hanan Aboulafia 20

Notes 23

for all emigrants who lost homes and family

How to Become an Emigrant

Live where barrel bombs destroy your home, parents, wife.

Hear rumors that the army suspects you don't obey their kill orders.

Pay the smuggler your black market $2,000 to get to Greece.

Acquire a small backpack—in it put

    one extra shirt, one pair of pants,
    plastic bag to keep them dry,
    waterproof box for bandages, cigarettes, matches,
        birth certificate, army papers,
    3 lemons to prevent dehydration,
    box of dates—2 per day for 10 days,
    painkillers in case your back goes out again,
    life jacket for when your boat gets rammed or sinks,
    sunscreen for days you spend bobbing in the sea,
    a laser pointer—your boat travels at night; if it sinks
        rescuers may find you by its light.

Pray.

At Sea with Laser Pointer

Akram's first mission—
kill the family who fed members
of al-Nusra, Islamic State enemies.

Dark at 10, he takes night vision binocs,
walks to their apartment,
kicks in the door,

beams the laser,
grandparents, parents, kids asleep on pallets.
Shoots each one with his pistol.

After the first shot the boy looks up at him.
About his younger brother's age,
same droopy left eye.

No choice,
he has to shoot.
Does.

Needs to get to Greece.
If he stays, al-Nusra kills him.
Leaves the pistol, night binocs.

Keeps the laser pointer.
If the overloaded boat sinks at night,
Akram hopes rescuers will see the beam.

What He Carries with Him

He safeguards his backpack like it's made of gold.
His name is Iqbal, skinny seventeen, left Kunduz
when the Taliban defeated Afghan forces, sure
he'd have to fight. Entered Turkey through Iran,
hid under snow when soldiers came, been stuck
in Van Province for months. Afghanis not welcome
here, he can't stay in Adiyaman Refugee Camp or any
of Turkey's 16 other camps, can't work, no rights.
No one speaks for Afghanis. Iqbal wants to get to Europe
via Greece. Besides shampoo, a pair of socks, a pair
of pants, toothbrush and toothpaste, his prized possession—
face whitening cream, wants to blend in once he gets to Europe.

The Field Outside Homs

Azara worried—her husband not yet
home. She knew about the field, feared
he lay there—bullet between his eyes.
Rumor: the Free Syrian Army named him
traitor—he hadn't killed the family allied
with al-Nusra, their enemy.

Next morning friends brought him home.
Azara washed him, wrapped him in clean cloth,
went with friends who carried his coffin
to the courtyard where the imam offered prayers.
She couldn't go to the cemetery where he would lie
facing Mecca in his grave—women not allowed.

In Zaatari

They owned five houses in Aleppo,
rented four. Bombs destroyed them,
Nizar's plumbing business.
They moved to Amman but he found no

legal work, afraid he'd be arrested.
So, refugee camp—
Nizar & Aziza, five kids, his mother & aunt,
together in the 204-square-foot trailer.

If they need the bathroom,
one latrine for every 40;
one shower, every 100.
Mornings when Aziza collects their daily bread

she sees Syria
a few miles away
across the border.
His mother has cancer, needs chemo,

the only time she's allowed to leave.
They want to be in Syria but if they return,
who dies when the next bomb falls?
His mother wants to die at home.

Outside the chain-link fence & locked gate—
salt-flecked soil.
Far beyond, an orchard, pistachio or olive trees.

In the Refugee Camp the Art Therapist Asks Surayya About Her Painting

Tell me about the two people lying on the ground, Surayya.

> *They died. They got shot.*
> *They're bleeding but they can't move.*

There's a man and a woman in your painting.
What is each one holding?

> *My mother is holding my baby brother in a baby carrier.*
> *My father carries a little suitcase with some lentils*
> *and dates and money.*

You painted a helicopter. What is it doing in your picture?

> *It's dropping bombs.*
> *A bomb hit our house.*
> *We were hiding at my auntie's house.*

I see a man holding a gun pointed at two people.
What's happening?

> *He's in the army and he's killing my best friend and*
> *her mother.*

Where are you in the picture, Surayya?

> *I'm hiding behind these concrete blocks from a*
> *bombed building.*

What happened to you and your family after this picture?

> *We came here to the refugee camp in Turkey.*

If you could have two wishes, Surayya, what would they be?

> *I wish our house was still there.*
> *I wish I get to grow up, be a big girl.*

Dead Man Carried Lentils from Market

The Journalist: Airstrikes over, black smoke
& flames engulf the narrow streets of al-Kallaseh
in northeastern Aleppo. People flee concrete
chunks hurtling from a building buckling at
its midpoint. Oh, my God, that's al-Sakhour
Medical Center, the last standing hospital
in the city. I've reported on this war six years
& never seen such horror. When the air begins
to clear, men & women dash toward it. They
carry sheets & shovels, dig at rubble, fling
concrete aside, dig deeper. They tug on long
arms, pull out an old man who still grasps
a bag split open, lentils spilling from it.
They listen to his chest, shake their heads,
wrap him in a sheet.

**

The Widow: I begged my husband not to go,
bombs exploding near our neighborhood. He knew
we needed lentils, knew I can't walk so he went
to market. A bomb found him, Allah's will be
praised. Friends brought him home. I washed
him, wrapped him in white linen. Now he waits
for them to carry him to his grave. I cried until
no more tears came. What of me? No one in Aleppo
to take me in. Our three sons, all dead.

Touching Air

The three-year-old—too-bright eyes
matchstick legs & arms, skull straining
against taut-skinned face…

The eleven-year-old pregnant by invading
soldiers, father killed her while she slept—
impure…

The widow, in a wheelchair, no one
to care for her, all three sons
dead in war…

The soldier carrying on one shoulder
his father, on the other, his son,
both dead…

Bulletins from a War Zone

The only dervish left in Aleppo,
he whirls, white skirts full, flowing,
arms outstretched,
one palm toward heaven,
the other toward earth.

His work is love—
for Allah, eternal and divine,
for the hereafter.
The dervish whirls and in his whirling,
hopes to meet Allah direct, chants
a mystic phrase to purify his heart,
his voice, a melodic rhythm.
The dervish whirls and prays—
Allah is One, is All.

Room intact despite mortar shells that tore out upper floors,
the dervish whirls in prayer,
focusing on, whirling toward
Allah everlasting.

***

Ahmad is lost in music—
Schubert or Jabri—
not sitting on a chair before his phonograph,
although he is;
as if not surrounded by plaster chunks,
smashed glass, broken window frames,
although he is.

White beard, white hair,
in Aleppo all his 70 years,
he doesn't plan to leave his place on earth
because of bombs.

He draws on his pipe,
tobacco briefly flaring red,
leans in to better hear the music.

The Emigrant

scrub pine and wild almond
a small gray bird
they were free
he'd served the sentence
his crime   teaching
children their language
Kurds like him
living in Syria
he placed left foot
fought pain
left side of his body
weak from polio

and he was falling
falling again into the dog-kennel-sized room
soldiers had thrust him into
after he'd been spied upon
his school declared a traitor's act
and so the tiny cell
where he could not stand
where he could only crouch
arms grasping knees
head on chest
12 hours   18   24
he feels urine leaking
no
he commands it
back inside
but urine spills
he is wet
the kennel is cold
no food
no light
after 72 hours he pounds on the metal door

I'll sign anything
hand me papers or kill me now
the door opens
7 sheets of blank paper and a pen
he signs

in a land not his
his own land not his
grasping one low fir bough
a single drop of water
falling on his head
one drop
one drop
one drop

Raqqa Syria to Crete

Riham's 19, Syrian, working in Egypt *all human beings are born free*
her own town bombed out *and equal in dignity and rights*

Egypt doesn't want her, tries to kidnap *they are endowed*
and send her back *with reason and conscience*

She decides to go to Europe *and should act toward one another*
pays $2000 for a spot on a fishing boat meant for 50 max, 1 of 500

in a spirit of brotherhood 4th day at sea: her boat sinks *everyone has the right to life* She can't swim. A man hands her a life ring,

she floats, corpses bobbing around her *liberty and security of person.*
A man swims to her, hands her his 9-month baby, asks her to save it.

He sinks. A woman swims to her, hands her an 18-month baby, asks her to save it. She sinks. *No one shall be subjected to torture*

No food or water for 8 days *or to cruel, inhuman*
Corpses black in the sea. Babies listless. She sees a plane,

waves frantically. 9th day: a ship comes, takes her and the babies
to Crete, to hospitals   *or degrading treatment or punishment*

The younger baby dies, the older lives, weeks later is adopted *all human beings are born free*   Riham survives *equal in dignity*

and rights wants to get to Sweden, go to college *and should act toward one another*   bring her family to safety   *in a spirit of brotherhood.*

Dust, Blowing in the Wind

Into Newton's laws of motion Boko Haram storms,
rifles smoking, kidnaps 276 girls, forces them
onto truck beds, tires raising red dust as they drive north.

The girls want to be teachers, nurses, doctors,
had been taking the physics test to enter college.
How to tend goats, grind sorghum, they know,

 want more. In Sambisa Forest the soldiers
hold the girls, sell them as slaves for the bride price
of $12, kill them if they refuse. In the first week

57 escape, 4 die, 219 sit cross-legged in heavy burkas.
They sleep with rattlesnakes & scorpions, drink
thin soup, watch, dread-filled, as other girls

are dragged into the bush, dreams dry as the dust
blowing in their eyes. Three years pass.
The government frees 21 girls, then 82 more.

After thin soup, rattlesnakes, rape, what remains?
And 113 girls still missing.

In the Sahara

A monitor lizard flicks its forked tongue
at a sand rat whose burrow disappeared
when a sandstorm blew the dunes above it

10 feet northeast. The monitor extends
its head, bites the rat's neck, begins to eat.
This land is shapely golden dunes against

blue sky, no landmarks except for the group
of people trudging single file, white shirts
reaching to their ankles, men turbaned,

women's heads wrapped in long white
scarves against the heat and blowing sand.
Some miles ahead, an oasis, a few

date palms. For days the people haven't
eaten, haven't found water, former homes
receding every mile but not the memory

of their huts burning, set on fire by soldiers'
torches, granary empty for months. Ahead
will be a village with cousins who may

take them in, share food. Near an old man's
foot, a scorpion stings a scarab beetle,
poison stilling it.

The Sahel

From savannah to Sahara, Senegal
to Sudan, our land, the Sahel. Ground
deep-fissured, drought-cracked, the few
plants withered without water, riverbeds
dry. Parasite-filled mud hole, dead
donkey, three dead cows, hides sun-dried,
stretched over bones. The sirocco
blows from the Sahara, swirls sand,
raises dust storms a half mile high.
Always, wind blows, sand drifts.
Always.

We are ghosts walking, so thin
our ribs protrude, our knees
swollen knobs between our sticks
of thighs. You do not see us.
We are too thin to see. All our lives
too little food, two ounces of grain
once a day. Always hungry. Our babies
cry themselves to sleep, our children's
bloated bellies scream. Sleep
hungry, wake hungry, walk
hungry. We are ghosts, walking.
Away from wind that always
blows, away from sand that
scratches faces, blinds our eyes.
Away from homes no longer
homes, crops dried, granaries
bare. We would walk to food
but where is that? Where *is* that?

One day soldiers   in the village
torched   our homes   I saw
the thatch   catch fire   grabbed
the baby   ran   No one
knew why   nowhere   to prepare
the daily meal   nowhere
to sleep

Early one morning   my mother   knew
something   bad   would happen
She called us   inside
told us   to crouch on the floor
not   to walk to school
Minutes later   soldiers
shot   everybody   outside

We heard   in other   villages
soldiers   killed people   in the fields
We   were afraid   to plant sorghum
village granary   empty   for months
One night   I was so thirsty   I pretended
my saliva   was a drink of water
no saliva came

The market's empty   Merchants
used to bring bright cloths   on camels
herders drove goats
farmers' donkey carts   loaded
with squash   onions   peppers
No one trades   anything
No one can trade   anything

One day   soldiers   They grabbed
my son   put a belt   of bullets
around his   neck   a pistol in his   hand
Said   he would   make a fine   soldier
He was 10   Is he   alive

My father was   outside   When he saw
soldiers   he turned his   head   hoped
they wouldn't see   him   They caught
him   chopped off   his hand
for disrespect

Three men   came   with guns
My daughter was   out   in the millet field
They   raped   her   hit   her head
Now she's   blind

Wind blows, sand drifts.
We ghosts are walking.
You do not see us.
We would walk to food, to safety.
But where is that?
Where *is* that?

Aseel Turned Away at Airport Gate

How I learn English? Hah! My older brother
study in American university, marry
American girl, come back to Baghdad.

They live in my parents' house two, three
years. She taught me to say English words
like she said, better than my college teacher.

I not good writing English—not pencil,
not pen, not computer. No! But speaking,
yes! Words run loose in my head, twist

and tilt, and then like dragonfly out of nymph,
my words come beautiful, like wild iris.
So I translate for two American soldiers

four, five years. My English so good
they say I save their lives so many times.
They wear very good helmets, Kevlar vests,

I wear shirt and cap. Ok, I don't be wounded.
But now my visa to come to America no good.
ISIS want to kill me, bleach my bones white

because I help American soldiers. They vultures,
want to pick my bones. What I do? I make plan B.
My buddy Omar train to be a pilot. I hide

in baggage, hop out when he land in Mosul,
follow River Tigris into Turkey. Then I be
safe. Maybe Turkey rainbow for me.

My Name Is Hanan Aboulafia
In memory of Syrians who didn't survive their emigration

When mortars screamed she crouched below
the window. Shells punched through walls
as if through cardboard, front door a black
hole gaping into night. The table where they'd
eaten lentils, plaster dust and splinters.
On the pallet where they slept, her baby
in her mother's arms, both crushed as the ceiling
fell. She lifted off heavy chunks of plaster,
closed Doua's eyes, her mother's eyes, held Doua,
so much blood, such a little body. The Islamic State.
Again. They shot her husband for a rebel, friends
carried him home to bury, then her father died,
heart attack. All her family gone. She's 19,
widowed, orphaned, her baby dead.

*   *

Widowed, orphaned, her baby dead, she can't
remain in Syria, no ceiling over her head,
no door to shut out night, food nearly gone.
She can't go to Egypt, Jordan, Libya—no
work, she has no skills except for wife
and mother. She can't stay here: she'd be forced
to marry again, but Syrian men don't want
widow brides. She can't marry outside
her tribe, Saudi or Turk. If she wed another
fighter, he'd be dead in months. She can't
go through that again. She can't stay here.
She'll sell her bridal jewels for cash, buy
a backpack, bring what she needs for a new
life. Pay someone to bring her to Greece.

*   *

Pay someone to bring her to Greece—sounds
easy. Three days she's sat on this gray dinghy
bailing water with a plastic cup, the boat not
made for 18 people—six sit on each side,
another six on the bottom. It rides too low.
The owner tells them *throw away your backpacks*.
She's willing, but she has to keep her cell phone—
the photo of her husband smiling at her in his
army uniform, the photo of her baby Doua's
first tooth. As they start to sink an old man
stands up, tells them, *I'm doing this to save
your lives*. He jumps, the water swallows him.
She stares at where he sank, his red bandana
floating still. The boat rides higher.

* *

Riding higher, the boat reaches Kos, fifth
night. They beach the boat in darkness, leave
lifejackets, find an overheated limbo of refugees
and tourists who resent them, who look away
from dirty hair, stained clothes, open sores.
At night they sleep on sidewalks, on flattened
cardboard pushed up against walls still warm
where by day merchants sell their wares.
Rotting orange peel, fish scales underfoot,
always dust, always wind, no bathrooms.
For food, the cafe's back door. Sometimes
a cup of lentils, a slice of bread. Not halal.
She has to eat. She's lost, one refugee among
thousands who seek new homes.

* *

One refugee among thousands, she has one chance. Today, the Kos police station. She'll ask for a permit to go to Athens, from there to whatever country will take her. Why do you seek asylum, they'll ask. Who persecutes you? *I don't want to be an Islamic State bride,* she'll say. *I don't want to be forced to service fighters. I have seen my father dead, the Islamic State killed my husband, mother, baby. I want to live. I deserve to live.* They will look at her. *I want to go to Germany, learn to be a nurse. Then I'll go to Jordan, help refugees in camps. Many wounded, such need. I need your help. My name is Hanan Aboulafia.*

Notes

These poems are based on research I conducted from 2014 to 2017. Sources include PRI, PBS, NPR, CNN, United Nations Security Council, United Nations Universal Declaration of Human Rights, TED Talks, New York Times, The Guardian, Washington Post, Al Jazeera, and talks given by a Syrian emigrant.

Page 9: Zaid Jabri is a famous contemporary Syrian composer.

Page 11: An emigrant from Syria who experienced the events in this poem asked that I not use his name.

Page 13: Italicized words come from the UN General Assembly's Universal Declaration of Human Rights, Articles 1, 3, and 5. The Syrian woman's story was told by Melissa Fleming in a TED talk (TEDxThessaloniki.19:15. Filmed May 2015).

Page 20: "My Name Is Hanan Aboulafia" is based on many articles I read about Syrian emigrants. No person I am aware of has the name of Hanan Aboulafia. I chose these names because of their meaning: *Hanan*, meaning *tenderness*, and *Aboulafia*, meaning *owner of the power*.

Though **Susan Shaw Sailer** has lived in the United States all her life, after seeing the terrible destruction in the Middle East and North Africa on evening news, she felt compelled to write about the suffering that people experienced there. Sailer read extensively to gather background material and then wrote the poems that appear in this volume.

www.ingramcontent.com/pod-product-compliance
Lightning Source LLC
LaVergne TN
LVHW041519070426
835507LV00012B/1674